MARLENE DIETRICH,
RITA HAYWORTH, &
MY MOTHER

Camino del Sol
A Latina and Latino Literary Series

Marlene Dietrich, Rita Hayworth, & My Mother

Rita Maria Magdaleno

THE UNIVERSITY OF ARIZONA PRESS

TUCSON

The University of Arizona Press

© 2003 Rita Maria Magdaleno

First printing

All rights reserved

♾ This book is printed on acid-free, archival-quality paper.

Manufactured in the United States of America

08 07 06 05 04 03   6 5 4 3 2 1

Library of Congress Cataloging-in-Publication Data

Magdaleno, Rita Maria, 1947–

Marlene Dietrich, Rita Hayworth, & my mother / Rita Maria Magdaleno.

p. cm. — (Camino del sol)

ISBN 0-8165-2258-8 (pbk. : alk. paper)

1. German Americans—Poetry. 2. Mothers and daughters—Poetry.
3. Germany—Poetry. 4. Arizona—Poetry. I. Title: Marlene Dietrich,
Rita Hayworth, and my mother. II. Title. III. Series.

PS3613.A3455 M37 2003

811'.6—dc21   2002004776

British Library Cataloguing-in-Publication Data

A catalogue record for this book is available from the British Library.

Publication of this book is made possible in part by the proceeds of a
permanent endowment created with the assistance of a Challenge Grant from
the National Endowment for the Humanities, a federal agency.

In memory of
Maria Kramer,
my mother

Contents

My Mother's Hair

When I think of my mother at seventeen, I see her
sitting on the floor of the warm kitchen
on Brunnenlechgässchen. It is 1946
and the war is over, a bright spring afternoon.
The earth has stopped trembling.
My mother has gotten a perm, curls shining
like copper. "Pretty girl," my father is singing
and dancing around her. "Yes,
you are my pretty girl," smell of bread
rising, calendulas on the table.
Martha, my mother's best friend,
is riding away on her motorcycle.
The war is over.
My mother's hair
is shining.

I

THE RED DOOR

Grenze
—Berlin, 1991

This damp Saturday morning, our train clicks
steady and slow, east to Berlin. I sit
with three old women, our small brown
compartment heavy with smoke. Two of these
women are from Augsburg and one of them
is my godmother, my German aunt; the other
woman comes from the east, Saalfeld.
They are smoking, drawing deeply on HB
cigarettes; they are discussing the reconstruction
of the east, last week Berlin hailed as the new
capital by a narrow margin of votes.
"We'll have to pay for everything," they mutter
and I watch the land slide green against
my window, an old village cemetery
suddenly standing up in thick wet grass.
Now we are pulling into Ludwigsstadt
and the east German woman is saying,
"Look! We are coming to the border."
She is beginning to tell us about
the long separation from her mother
who lives in the west, Erlangen. She
is explaining how they were split
by the border, *die Grenze,* for more
than forty years. Now we are stopping
in Probstzella, border town where I go
to an open window, lean out and look
for remnants of the old wall. Here,
I can imagine the way *die Polizei* guarded
this famous line of freedom. Here, I can see

how that sharp division between east and west
has already fallen away. Here, I see a solitary
finch and the old faces of gray houses staring
back at me. Here, I can feel an old separation—
of heart and land, of mother and daughter. This
trip is like going back more than forty years
and I'm thinking of my dead mother, of the borders
we once constructed between one another.

But now Germany speaks
of reunification and all of us—
mother and daughters—are traveling
freely from west to east across
die Grenze, wet border. She is
wide open like a mother
who is ready
to give birth.

Sophie and the White Rose
—Munich

Sophie and her brother, Hans, were young students at the University of Munich. They were members of the White Rose Movement, an anti-Nazi resistance group. May 1943, they were charged with treason and executed by guillotine.

Don't call me a heroine; I'm dead.
I studied biology and philosophy.
My brother, Hans, was in medicine.
He wanted to be a doctor.
I begged him, *Let me work*
for the White Rose.
He said, *It is better*
not to know some things.

1942
White Rose, White Rose I sang
in my head as I washed the windows,
fixed the morning coffee, brushed
my long brown hair, fed Mitzi
our white cat. *White Rose,*
Oh let me work for the White Rose!
I sang and sang.

In March, the bombs
began falling
like failed stars
on the city.

5

❧

Finally, Hans relented.
It was July and we stood
in the heart of the city
with Christof, my brother's friend.
Under the linden trees, we
planned our first subversive
act. The trees, breathing
green, kept our secret.

❧

Die Weihnacht, 1942,
a Christmas without light.
Nearly a new year,
no gifts, no tree,
little Star of David,
glimmer of hope, who
will say the truth?

1943
It was a bright, cold morning
in February. We scattered
our pamphlets throughout
the lecture halls, an explosion
of paper from so many
windows, the truth whirling
like snow, *White Rose,*
White truth.

❧

Slush of memory, ice
on the gray window ledge,
March the 4th. Hans stamping
his feet in the doorway; he
was saying, *It's true,*
they have started
sending people
to the death camps.

All that spring,
the chestnut trees
were full of tight green
buds ready to burst
open like me.

We were arrested
in May. At the Palace
of Justice, our judge
wore scarlet robes.
We got a hasty trial;
the final verdict:
guilty of treason.

Hours before the execution,
our mother, Magdalene
arrived from Ulm.

She was crying; I tried
to console her. *Mutti,*
tell me about the garden,
your roses—the red ones,
and the beautiful white ones.
Will they be blooming in June?
Tell me, Mutti.
Will they?

Memorial Walk
  —Dachau, 1991

The linden trees are green
umbrellas standing
in the heart of Dachau,
pretty rows held
in perfect formation.

Fifty years ago, no one
in town would ever
say *concentration camp* or
deportation train, fire, bullet,
lack of bread & shoes.

The people who planted
these trees have disappeared.

"Only an adjustment
of their political attitude;
that's what they got
at Dachau. That's what
we believed to be true,"
my godmother Resl
is telling me. Still,
she fears the truth.

It is raining, late
summer, one hundred
black umbrellas
resisting a lead-gray
sky. Stone words

are telling us,
Never again
and the trees
are greener
than we could
ever remember.

The Red Door
   —Augsburg, 1941

This morning, the small cries
of children. Sometimes,
I hear them running
into first light,
the school yard quiet
as a boneless fish, split
river, the sudden escape
of birds and leaves spilling
red-blue on a path
to the school door.

Rotes Tor, my mother called
it, *Red Door,* her grade school
full of mirrors and apples,
the half-composed letters
of children, crude Gothic script
before Hitler sent young girls
to farm camps. There
my mother peeled potatoes,
wiped the first blood
smearing her inner thighs,
her brother on a submarine
that never surfaced.

What do we call this memory
of death, this grief of children?
I remember the way my daughter
at two would suddenly appear
at the screened door, breathless.

How the wind circled her
and carried the faint smell
of fire. How my Oma
told my mother not to be afraid
the morning she stepped
into that truck full of girls
leaving for camp,
the door of their school
shut like a large red eye.
How everything we believe
can begin to fall away
like apples loose in the bed
of a pickup or birds splitting
their wings across farm fields.

Somewhere on another farm,
I imagine children
climbing
the evening porch.
Silently, they wash
the dust from their hands,
go in for milk
and supper.

Firestorm
    —Hamburg, July 27, 1944

Fear not, for I have redeemed you, I have called you by name . . .
when you walk through fire you shall not be burned and the flame
shall not consume you.—Isaiah 43:2

The fire reached 1000 degrees,
trees gliding out of the earth
like kindling, the city blind
with light, children
bursting
into bright candles,
Whoosh, the smallest
disappearing
completely.

A nameless sea
of faces, his
captured
most clearly,
the dazzling moment
he was torched,
bone fused
to metal,
a skeleton
pedaling
the charred
bike, Gandalf

the Wizard
falling
into the Crack
of Doom.

Blonde hair rose
into green auras,
the eerie warning
no one understood.
Too late,
brilliant crowns
of light already
crackling
above the flaxen
heads of the innocent;
Holy Ghost
where were you?

Red city, red night
falling on the multitude
rising in that fire-
wind. Was it
beautiful,
those bodies
taking flight?
It was July,
their dazzling
ascension into hell,

the body finally
learning
how to fly.

Gandalf the White,
Wizard of the Inferno,
you took the charred soul
of the city, mine
still roaring
in the flames,
a Phoenix bird,
alas y restos,
birdwings
& ashes
in my heart.

Experiments in Hypothermia

on the prisoners of Dachau
found nothing conclusive

except that it was necessary
to plunge the freezing person

into warm water right away;
more than sixty died in the water

tanks in Dachau; this happened
in 1945, barely two years

before I was born down
the road in Augsburg.

Salzbergwerk: The Salt Mines Tour

At two, our bus leaves Mirabell Platz,
heart of old Salzburg, "Salt Fortress,"
city surrounded by *Kurgartens,* castles
and Mozart's little birth house, the Salzach
River running deep, gray blue. This route
will take me through the Bavarian Mountains
and Obersalzberg, Hitler's mountain retreat,
his second headquarters. Here, I am traveling
alone past the Königsee Valley, farmhouses
and ruins. Here, I am crossing wet green
land and moving back into Germany, tour
to the Salt Mines of Berchtesgaden,
450 years old, this journey back
to my Mother.

At Berchtesgaden, I will put on miner clothes,
the muslin pants, the coarse black jacket.
There, I will follow the movement of Anna
Karolina Sohr, my grandmother who came
to these salt mines in 1938 with Sep,
her young son who would become a soldier
and die in Potsdam in 1945, a final stand
against the Allies. At Berchtesgaden, I will
travel deep into the salty tunnel. There,
I will take a 100-foot-long slide into the grottos;
there, I will ride a raft and glide inside
the glistening womb of rock and salty water;
there, I will learn about the origin of salt.
And I will begin to understand that it takes
at least one year to drill into a good spot,

to make careful preparations, to probe
and to analyze each sample
before any drilling begins.

Always, there is water: to draw out
the salt, to wash and to cleanse.
At Berchtesgaden, I will know
that salt mining takes time and patience,
takes so much tapping, carefully
tapping to make sure a new spot
is stable and capable of releasing
the salt—"White gold"—
from that womb
of rock and black water.

Little Universe

The silent world is our only homeland. —Francis Ponge

Dachau, little universe
of pain, white spike of a star,
a child's face in snow,
another slumped across a wire

fence, swish of memory, *why*
did we forget their names?
"They are still here,"
the guide is saying, our group

circling the camp, the brown
records, that exactness of rations:
One half-liter of coffee;
two hundred fifty grams

of bread, soup, fear, hole
in the heart. Experiments
of centrifugal force, the body
spinning apart, the terrible

need to know the moment a heart
gives up gravity and hope.
Small universe of pain
glistening red in the marrow

of my bones, the wish
to reconcile a truth:

I was born thirty-six kilometers
from Dachau, this

memory more difficult
to shape
than the blood
on frozen snow.

High Summer

It's high summer, *hochsommer*.
Tonight, the moon will float up
fat and yellow over the Bayerischen
Wald, miles and miles of heavy green
hills. This evening I'm on a bus
coming back from Prague, Golden City
where we ate *Schnitzel mit Rahmsosse,*
and *Knödel,* where we sat at long tables
packed with tourists, where we drank
cognac and dark beer, where I admired
our waiter, his thick black mustache
and heavy shoulders. There
I paid a woman ten korunas
to get tissue and a toilette.
I remember how she handed each
of us a small square of paper
after we dropped enough coins
into her small white ashtray.
Her head was wrapped
in a blue scarf.

It's high summer in the Golden City,
Prague overloaded with tourists
who comb the castle, cathedrals,
and a cemetery of Jews, dead
since 1400. It's high season
and the river spills wide
through the city; a small gypsy
boy stands on the bridge and plays
"Red River Valley" on a keyboard;

the mime moves slowly in bright
pink and black; a banner
flies white: "Franz Kafka—
IMAGINE! Light Show."

It's high summer and the men are selling
ouzo at a roadside table as we travel
back to the German border. Cows graze,
slow color of mocha coffee and cream,
an occasional flock of chickens. Earlier
we stopped near Hlinsko to buy cherries
from a woman who stood in a heavy
white apron, her daughter in blue jeans.
I could see the red tips of this woman's
fingers and we bought cherries,
all of them, three small trees
near our bus. Finally, each one
stripped, picked clean.

It's high summer and we're coming
to the border, our shopping bags full
of cherries, *Oblaten,* ouzo and duty-free
cartons of Marlboros. I'm thinking about
that mother, how she stood empty-handed
beside her daughter, how they watched
our silver bus pull away, quickly.
Now the sun drips orange behind wild
hills curving all around us
and I wonder what is left
for that woman to give her daughter
besides a small space at that roadside
stand, to sell cherries. And sometimes
to get cheated by people like us,

tourists who need to take something
home, who expect to travel with full
pockets across the border. High
summer, the moon swelling up
fat and yellow over the border.
Over each row of naked
cherry trees.

The Ride

Through the medieval city,
the Danube runs with amber light;
here, a museum of belts
and nails, documents
of women tortured. *Yes,*
they would've got you, too,
says Oliver, my cousin.
        We ride
a border of the forest's heart,
narrow road shining, the dark
hills hunkered down, caves
and cottages where the women
lived. *Yes, that's where they stirred*
their spells, his hand waving,
spill of red geraniums in window
boxes. We enter the dark green
heart, my cousin rolling up
the windows, a light rain coming.
Would've got you, those birthmarks
on your face, the sign of being
a witch, he whispers. We speed on,
blur of yellow European
road signs.
    Late afternoon
we stop for a good coffee
& cognac; I smoke HB cigarettes,
breathe deeply, consider
the glass casket of fairy tales
learned as a child. *Yes, they*

would've got you, words falling
like crimson light into the trees,
into the hushed air.

Standing Torture
    —February 1942

There was snow
        on the night
the men stood

in white
        formation

there was snow
        all night
in Dachau.

Schutzstaffel, SS Uncle

Luis, I never knew you, seen more coldly
in this winter light. You had a decent life.
Your mother, now dead, called you
my damp rose. Your brother still searches
for you, never wanted to admit you were
the one who hid the tattoo, that stark symbol
fired into the pit of your arm.
You were cruel;
the song of light never entered your throat,
and the Aryan blood I carry is tinged blue,
the sky grieving a sea of shining skulls,
a cruel streak
silver as the oar of a boat drifting on a lake of bones.

Brunnenlechgässchen, the small source street
is where you began to feel yourself opening, but the horror
grew daily and you became a fist punching the gray sky.

You were the one who hated dark ones. Would you have hated
me too? I'm not hiding in the sacred plumes
of a white swan, blonde boy
you were the one plucking the heads of doves
there at the creek with your father.
If they knew the truth
of this dying century, the Hungarians would hand you over.
Uncle, traitor, SS, gunner, killer, exterminator of all that was,
how many times did you refuse to say, *"It ends now"*?

If the world holds your redemption, white flower of truth
conceived in darkness, I cannot find it,

der Bayerische Marsch marsch marsch!
black boots, goose-stepping
Einundzwanzig, zweiundzwanzig,
twenty-one, twenty-two
marching marching, *zwanzig, zwanzig,*
dreissig, vierzig
twenty thirty forty more
to kill. White flag of surrender,
I want to stake it into your heart.

Luis, I am waiting at the winter river, branch
of a linden tree shining in my Azteca
heart, mixed blood you would have
spilled without hesitation,
Schutzstaffel, SS uncle,
I am waiting for you.

Memorial
 —for Alois Kramer

1

1947, European spring, season
of reconciliation, reconstruction,
you serving up your war stories
on a table wiped clean for your
toothless friends, smell of cigars
and sweat, three dead sons.
You are waving your hands
across your memories.

2

France, 1962, a crest of white
crosses, half a century of forgotten
dates. The soldiers are sleeping
under soft moss, pale sun crawling
over each green plot and your son,
Fritz. Finally, you are claiming
his small lost grave.

3

During the war, German nuns
baptized the babies
so they wouldn't go to Limbo,
holy sacrament
of Baptism, water trickling
over each
bloody head.

4

Opa, I remember the dead
rabbit, a bony creature,
barely enough to feed us.
You cracked the spine,
exposed a network
of nerves; I saw
burned flesh,
glass stars, blown-
out windows,
a field of flax
whirling inside
that fragile column
of bones.

5

Sometimes, I still sit by the window
while everyone sleeps, red shawl
on my shoulders, the wind
spinning up memories. *Yes,
the war, so many sins,*
Ana was saying. *Bitch,*
you sputtered; never
forgave her. Years,
she waited for a knock
at the door from Luis,
her brother, your son
who never came home.

6

Old man, you had to gum
your stories, teeth and lies
dropping out one by one,

milk bread in a bowl,
white mush. You kept
secrets in the cellar,
in the dark, you
entering my mother
at ten; you rising
each time I hear
the black boot
stamp my doorstep.

Anna Karolina Travels to Andilly, France
to Claim Her Missing Son
    —September 28, 1962

Against a backdrop of dark
green grass, I see you surrounded
by a pale sea of headstones,
two to a grave, cold
cement crosses, your
thick black coat,
scuffed shoes,
one big button
riding your breastbone,
broken heart, short
fingers, your working
hands, pillbox cap
on your head,
the dead soldier
under your feet.

Eighteen years, you
waited for this
day, bucket of white
roses you brought
for the boy, Friedrich
you loved him.

The poplar trees
stood quietly,
witnessed your
reclamation;

the trees,
they had waited
so long.

The War Bride
  —for Ana Kramer, 1946

    After the war,
the gypsies returned
to Augsburg. They
pitched their dark camp
at the edge
of the Seven-Tabled
Forest.
    The girl wished
to have her cards
read. It was winter
and her mother said
it would be a sin.
    She waited
for a knock at the door,
a woman arriving
in lilac scarves.
    The gypsy saw
a wedding, a journey
over water, the snow
in Pennsylvania, blonde
children yet to come.
    The mother
began to cry.

To Market

That winter morning, you traveled with your mother to the *Vogelmarkt*
in Augsburg, red smell of slaughtered birds, the war years ending.
It was 1925 and you wore sapphire earrings, the gift passed down
from Tante Rose, your mother's aunt. You sat on a little box
in the market; Anna Karolina, your mother, was selling eggs.
Ana, you were five and the earrings shone like two chips of stars
around your blonde hair, beautiful. A man ripped away the sea-blue
jewels; your earlobes bled. And your father continued to raise, to kill
chickens. That thick red smell, the limp throats, the wet
feathers; you never forgot. You grew to hate those birds and your father
who did not love your mother.

Another morning, in June, there is cool green air stirring
around the Green Dragon flea market. And the news
of a small tornado rising up, ripping out the oak trees
near the Susquehanna River. You walk slowly, at seventy-five,
light another cigarette before the rain arrives. Your daughters
are clustering around you, their black umbrellas
opening, the heavy sugar-smell of funnel cake
and cream. *Let's wait it out, Mom,* your oldest girl
whispers, the storm whipping closer, the dark smell
of coffee, the tent billowing like a big white ship
ready to sail. *Such a sweet cake,* you say, the rain
more violent, the daughters you wanted to love.

Second Tour
   (for the fifty-sixth anniversary of the liberation of Dachau,
   29 April 2001)

In the photo, men are gathered
for deportation. A blonde boy
with a black cap is the one I notice:
square chin, the dark & clear eyes
that appear to be staring into a country
of unlit tapers & broken menorahs.
He was handsome, I tell my daughter.
The smell of snow descends

Rub it for good luck, Georg tells me
at the fountain in the *Marktplatz,*
Nürnberg, Good Friday, a meatless
day. He points out the golden ring
& I touch it, pose for a photo. Later,
my aunt, Rosamie, serves us two pieces
of strudel & extra vanilla sauce,
the white bowls rimmed in silver;
yes, we should enjoy
the good things in life,
she smiles

I am waiting for the low clouds
on the meadow to lift, for my SS uncle
to come home

❧

In the emerald silence
of a beautiful spring, like this one,
men waited
for their ration
of bread & coffee

❧

Clean it up, she ordered my mother,
blood clots of a girl's menses
floating in the clogged latrine,
spring 1945, the work camp,
the mistress holding a gun
to my mother's head. *Clean it up
yourself,* my mother answered,
& all the young girls clustered
in the doorway; *kill me & you'll
have to kill us all.* The girls
stayed, pressed closer, a shaking
muscle in the wrist, the mistress
pulling the gun slowly away.
A blue star beating
in my mother's temple

❧

In the dream, I am standing
in a doorway, heap of lilies
in my arms. A blonde boy
in the black & white photo
appears. He tells me his name:

Marcus Kowler, yes,
Marcus, like Mark,
the straight line of his mouth
breaking into a map
I will follow

❧

After all the fields have been
harvested, the girls will come home,
white kerchiefs on their heads.

Those Red Tulips

No one ever escaped from Dachau. —Alison, our tour guide,
14 April 2001

Her soft British accent, pale and earnest
face, red hair cropped against the gray sky.
Clouds lower and we huddle closer together,
smell of snow in the air. I breathe into my hands
to keep warm, my daughter leans into the story:

"Gerber daisies, lilies, violets and tulips grew
profusely. Right here by the poplar trees. Yes,
this is where the flower gardens bloomed. They
were tended by the camp prisoners, the flowers
gathered and wrapped into bundles to be sold

in the *Stadtmarkt,* for the people in the city
of Dachau. They were beautiful. They moved
freely through the gate, past the wired electrical
fence, the rifles, the dogs, the cold fast current
of water churning around the camp. The flowers

moved freely past the infirmary, past the men
lying ill with typhus, past the dead, the bones, the cold
water experimental tanks, the pole-hangings. The flowers
held secret places inside their damp folds, messages
tucked into the petals, smuggled out of the camp.

Words rode deeply inside those flowers, truth
of the sick, a note stuffed into the tulips: *We are suffering*

beyond belief, the typhoid barracks, the men lying naked
or in their underwear, no care for them. I am afraid
it is too late for us. Samuel Weise, 29 May 1942.

Frau Lotti Hayter, a sympathizer, carried the small bundle
of red tulips down Augsburger Strasse, hurried home
and climbed the dark stairs. She snipped the brown
string binding the stems, news of the dead
falling on her supper table."

Poppies

red survivors
waving

at the window
of our train

slipping out
of Berlin.

II

Marlene Dietrich,
Rita Hayworth, & My Mother

First Photograph of My Mother after the War, 1947

When the walls and cobblestones
in Augsburg finally stopped
trembling, your mother cried.
But you pulled your dark hair
out of your eyes, pinned it
back for this photographer
on Hoettner Strasse. Now
he is arranging our faces
white against a cane-backed
chair for the photo you will
mail to an American soldier
you say is my father.
My fists hold your fingers
tight, as the photographer
angles your chin, tilts it
until your face rises
softly into the lens.
Your eighteenth year
finally starting
to focus in
more clearly.

Marlene Dietrich, Rita Hayworth, & My Mother
  —1946

PFC, smart in that khaki
uniform, she fell in love
with your wide smile
& thick black hair,
glint of a gold tooth
like a star or a broken
promise you still carry.
How easy it seemed
you fell in love, your
baby sister saying,
She's too purty!
Marlene Dietrich pretty,
her smoky voice
& those wide Aryan
eyes that promised
never to lie, bore you
a child she named Rita.
Yes, after Rita Hayworth
she said that balmy eve
you left the movie theater
at the Sheridan Kaserne,
arm in arm. *My pretty girl*
you called her and summer
was ending, chestnut trees
lining the sidewalk
of Königstrasse, King Street,
the untranslatable language
of love. Mexican American
GI with your pretty girl,

you were the one who wanted
that Hollywood film
to go on & on. You
still recasting
its beautiful ending.

The Three Leonas
    Performing at the Sheridan Kaserne
    —Augsburg, 1946

You stand in a scatter of stars,
the blue curtains shimmering,
silky sky, the stage
full of light and the sleeves
of your costume billowing
like two small ships
wavering toward
a bright horizon, America.
Tonight, you wear blue
& gold, your small moment
of fame, you shining
on stage, applause
of the NCOs.
You have learned
to balance
a man on the crown
of your head, to survive
postwar Europe, your
mother still mourning
three dead sons.
Tonight, you bend
easily into each position,
tighten and release each
strand of muscle—*trapezius,
deltoid, bicep*—your body
glimmering and curving,
a lucky horseshoe.
Finally the last round

of applause streams
onto the stage
and you take a bow,
your face already
rising, moon
in the harbor,
New York, your
immigrant dream.
    (for my mother)

My Mother Riding the Morning Train
Just Before the End of the War

It was that long-standing quarrel of the onion fields and the lack of milk
in a country just before the war ended, the drone of American planes
above the trees and how the sound ripped open. Yes, that's the way

the plane swooped over us. I was going to work in the next town,
Ulm, and the bullets flew on the roof of the commuter train like an angry
god, a rain of fire. He cried, *get down, get down,* the man in a gray coat

beside me pushing my head under the seat. A red scream split open
another world; it was the day I believed in hell, the boy running
past my window, the boy with his back on fire and the man pushed me

harder under the wooden seat. His hand on my head, my father pushing
the cellar door open, the room cool, the damp smell of onion and
something saltier, too. The belt buckle was cold like the extinguished stars

above St. Ulrich's cathederal, my father's hand pressing the back
of my head, *there, hold it there,* his knee and the famine coming close,
closer. Until there was nothing left inside my stomach, the milky

dreams of orphan children curdled in my mouth, songs
of the fatherland escaping from the bullet-riddled train.

Maria on the High Wire

It is what you always wanted, and so I imagine it now:
you rising into the center of this sky-blue circus,
your rhinestone tiara, the sunlight radiating
in your hair, flight of your hands. Then,
it is more insistent, your desire to spin
something beautiful at the edge of war,
the curve of a question mark, the Bavarian
peak where angels once converged & called
your true name; not Ria, but Maria,
the sound of linden trees aching into blossom
in Augsburg, Munich, Berlin, all the broken
cities, my father's matrimonial speech,
marry me, please. This magnification
of memory, of what we recall to be true.
There, your acrobatic stance, your shoulders,
your strong defiant chin, the clavicles
arched upward. There, you are taking
your rightful place, your name,
your sudden ascension into the glittering
lights. Below, the colonnades
of dark faces turned upward
like admiration or grief,
my father's jealous heart
on a chair.

The Sisters of Mercy

When I arrived, it had stopped snowing.
German nuns rose from their cots
like vesper sparrows fluttering
out of white nests,
my mother's breath escaping
from the yellow room
where other women labored.
It was spring, the fatherland
still soaked in blood, wet
mouths of the young
waiting to be fed. The nuns
were singing my mother's
penance: to birth me
without analgesics,
her sin for delivering
una hija natural,
illegitimate child
the Sisters of Mercy
prayed for, baptized
me quickly.

Arizona Photo of My Mother & Father, 1948

Halfway between Tucson & Phoenix
the plum shade of a saguaro

the way it becomes a prop
& the mainstay for the newlyweds

who pose at the base & smile
shining faces

her black Greta Garbo hat
his tipped smile

late afternoon leaving Tucson
heading home

no honeymoon
the long slow whine

of 16-wheelers heading to LA
the green promise held

in their mouths
till death do us

& how it would
be broken.

Falling in Love with Ludwig

You left for love on another continent,
your desire running like fissures
in a fault line you never noticed.

He washes my hair, you said,
his promises already fluttering
away, birds in a gray thicket.

Pay attention to the snow,
I wanted to tell you, that winter
on the other side of the world.

Let's go for a walk, you said,
the birds are leaving. Too late.
Wasn't I good enough? you asked.

First Light

Morning rounds, they call
your cancer *Krebs,*
a leap in the sounds
of language, movement
of light on your hands,
the snow and your hair
falling.

These clues you left:
A pressed four-leaf clover;
the half-crocheted blanket;
lucky numbers tucked
into your red wallet;
directions for playing
blackjack; a coin purse
full of American dimes
& quarters; your secret
summer of chemotherapy.

Now, early morning
I am bathing your face
and feet, soft breasts,
heart space, cunt
swollen like a newborn,
sound of a train
sifting across the Donau,
snow. Late
December, sky
and land dissolving
gray-white into

one another. Silence,
moment I will begin
to speak
two languages.

Hospice

That final round
of chemotherapy,
your hair falling
and winter coming

In the forest beyond
the city, ice crystals
gathering, your heart
distracted, the way

You could not sing
the truth, *a cigarette*
you said, your death shining
in the window

The snow beginning
vespers at six
so much for commitment
you wanted to say

To the nuns already
singing, you hurrying
past the hospital
window.

Kleine Gesten, Small Gestures

You are sleeping beside me
without memories, candles
and the smell of cinnamon tea
on the stove, silk, music,
skin, moonlight running
across my window ledge
in November, month before
my mother's death. You are sleeping
beside me without memories, brief
lover, night smells. Cinnamon
and sweat, the fierce way
I loved you slowly, your head
nesting in my elbow, my mother's
breath still warm, dark bird
in my memory. The wish, my longing
that would make your hand unfold,
wing brushing my cheek, delicate.

It is always the small gestures
which make us human—mothers
combing their daughters' hair;
washing a child's hands; gathering
red clover and jasmine for sun tea,
leaves heavy and wet. Mother,
the memory of you came today
in a small card, reprint, *In the Garden,*
mother and child, oil on canvas, a gift,
your childhood friend writing to me,

I remember so well, your mother with you
in her arms as we sent her off, the train
station, 1947, my god, where has time gone?

Night is spilling into the window, generous
air, chapparal quivering in the arroyo,
a clump of stars hovering above the house.
At dawn, moonlight will scatter yellow
through brittlebush and my heart
will crawl out of its cove
of grief, your hands moving
quietly through my dark hair.

Embroidering

(A Response to *Somnad,* by Carl Larsson)

A vase of hydrangeas on the table, this room
blue and clear, everything solid
and in its place. Here, two women
sit together, their knees
touching, stroking the beautiful
threads. One is pale green
like a single blade of weed
at the edge of a small pond. Another
strand is the color of deep wood
roses, wild and very sweet.
Also, threads like filaments
of fish tails, gold
and a blue string curled
like a child's ball, color
of sky on early desert mornings.

This afternoon, pale
and warm, the daughter listens
to her mother's breath, soft
and steady like a small animal
full of milk, nearly asleep,
this rhythm of breathing and needles
sliding slowly through the cloth.
They have planned this thing,
a tablecloth to spread out
for guests who will come
to this room, who will sit
and bow their heads to the white
plates of food. This will become

a cloth to be passed through
generations, needle of the mother,
needle of the daughter crossing
the cloth over and over.
A choreography of hands
and needles, and the daughter
wonders how this cloth
will sing.

Green Morning in the Summer Forest

Hummingbirds appear—I think of my mother,
emerald trees, hushed air, the sun
measured one hand above the horizon;
in the dream,
a gift, black
stockings, silk & rare,
a fine black line that ran the back
of each firm calf. Black
market, ration cards, *It took a lot*
of them to get one nice pair, she told
her friend who chose
a nubbier texture, good warm soil
in June, asters & daisies
sprouting easily under her hands.

The smoky nightclub
on Haunstetten Strasse,
exotic, emerald earrings,
the GIs whispering, *Come here*
& I will tell you how beautiful
you are, gin & tonic,
American martinis.

The hummingbird's emerald chest
glistens in morning, sting

of the black ant,
black tickets of love.

&

My mother's leaving
& leaving again for those smoky
nightclubs, her need
to be loved & loved
& loved, each night,
her beautiful legs.

&

The hummingbird & its partner, scarlet
throat, appear above the wooden deck,
hard *whirr* of wings descending;
then, the sudden, abrupt ascension
into the green morning, frantic
hearts, their love.

About My Mother's Ashes

Everything has disappeared into the earth,
you write from Nürnberg, *everything—*
the black skirt, the white blouse,
the leaves which made the tree
green and beautiful. *Everything has
disappeared—*the black shoe, the white
sock, the hair, the girl's smile, twigs
beneath her feet, weeds and wildflowers,
my mother's hand, darkness shrouding
the hillside, 1946. There, two girls
are posed together, arm in arm,
Siebentischwald, the forest
place, summer in Augsburg,
the wet green memory
assembling. There, my mother
and Martha, best friends,
their blouses growing
luminous in the heart
of an old photo.

*Everything has disappeared
into the earth,* you say, *even the urn,
yes, an official statement
from the cemetery administration.*

Georg, I say, you are the boy who stoked
coals for a quarter, for the GIs
on the Haunstetten Strasse, for the soldier
who was my father and you told him,
yes I have a sister; I say you are

the boy who didn't go to war
like your brothers & Resl, older sister
who fled Paris just before the Allies
arrived; I say it was my mother
who foraged sticks of wood,
hauled the frozen garbage
with your mother; I say
you are the one who wanted
to forget he had a dark sister
the day she said *get out of here,*
crystal curse, morphine
drip, stain of memory;
you never kissed her.

Nothing
has disappeared, I say.

Disappeared
    —Nürnberg, 2001

It was Resl, your sister
searching & calling an old friend
in Munich, 1990; he told her
Yes, Luis, a life in Hungary;
it is possible, everything
new; this is all I can say;
now, forget it. Now
your three sisters are dead;
and you, Georg, youngest
brother, sit at the table. *Yes,*
I went to Budapest, 1991;
that was a mistake.
How would we have known
one another since the war
ended? I was fourteen;
now, my hair is white.
The Danube was beautiful
& I remember that ride
through the hot city, late
June. I felt the gray
ghost of my brother riding
beside me. The sky
above Budapest broke
into thin-blue pieces,
an unsolved puzzle.

In your house, we sit
by the sliding glass
door, sip cognac. Uncle,

I ask for the truth. You
say, *Yes, one of the elite*
SS. My brother, Luis.

April snow is dusting
the gazebo, a scatter
of seeds for the birds. You
smooth the checkered tablecloth,
my eyes following that repetition
of squares, how precisely it is
all laid out before us,
a field of red coffins.
I trace the perimeter
of your sorrow. *Well, he is*
probably dead now, or perhaps
it is true that he has a new wife,
a new life in Budapest.
Yes, I'd hoped to find him;
probably dead, yes.
It's been so long,
gauze of light
and grief, your
defeated face,
late afternoon.
The unexpected
April snow.

The Leaving

Everywhere, the fragile smell
of rain. And despite the fact
that we were optimistic
about our future, the European
river still pulled me away

like Llorona. Then I
dressed in white, drank
only black coffee, took
a dark lover. Slowly I began
to understand the variously

sensitive scars in my memory.
When a dark ship arrived,
I entered that water. Finally I
understood the possibility
of finding the way home.

There, I imagined the child
I loved waiting patiently
at the table, her small
hands opening
to receive bread
and milk.

The Song

Tonight in your house, you sing
and it disappears when it wants to

like moon or star, jupiter glimmering
in a plum sky. There is no place

large enough to sleep with it,
room to room, a flurry of angels

recalling the gift of gifts; you
are not responsible for it, or

the smooth air, the way it remembers
everything, remembers you.

When the world falls in around you
and rocks sing a great distance,

you could wake up filled
with the possibility of something

essential to keep, your bones
turning phosphorus, something

to hold in your hands; the light
of particular moments

imbuing everything
you touch.

I Am the Daughter

of wind and wheat fields, daughter
of a crystal mother, of bombs

and submarines, of black land
and church spires, of music

in the mountains, daughter
of the edelweiss and the whore.

I am slicing dark bread, spreading
pale butter, blessing myself

with water from the marble font
in St. Ulrich's cathedral

Augsburg two thousand years old,
cobblestones and holy pain,

daughter who has lived *an der Donau,*
in the linden tree,

on Königstrasse,
on the Tegernsee,

on the Achensee, daughter
of a fairy tale mother,

who dreamed for hundreds of years
in a glass casket, who rode ships

on the Rhine and watched clear stars
rise on warm summer nights

until 1947, after the war, alien
daughter I crossed blue

mountains and water, wetback
in the New York Harbor,

wetback of a German mother,
Hosanna! Alleluia! Water,

holy, alien bitch, mother
and child, regal, we are

singing our way to America,
music and history

escaping
wet blue

from stained
glass windows.

Meditation on a Walk under the London Bridge
in Lake Havasu City, Arizona

Black fish are swimming in cool darkness.
This early April morning, I walk the river bank,
think of the jilted, the distraught, the ones
who dove off this gray transplanted arch,
the bass, their bodies floating—
dark clouds—soft
& transient as the hopes
of lovers, my mother

Lovely, the shadows
of those poplar trees at Dachau
in the spring, their deep
tunnels of color & grief

One black butterfly hovered
against the stained-glass windows.
Augsburg, morning after the New Year,
1990, my cousin Gerda saying *yes,*
it's your mother, the noiseless
sound of wings, the requiem
mass, eulogy, the priest clapping
incense higher & higher,
the snow

Say a prayer for her,
my father is calling forty years after
the divorce papers arrived & he broke down
crying, the gray angel
rising into his sleep, into all the tomorrows he would
live without her

{❤

Meet me at the headstone, bring some roses
I tell him. *I'm afraid to fly, honey,*
don't think I'll ever go back, he says.

Liberation Day

It is so many years before a war is over.
—from "Sweeping," by Naomi Ayala

The fugitive self returns
& explains how much
it has changed, how it freed
the child from terror,
how they sat down
quietly for soup
at the evening table.

Christmas 1989
—after the fall of the Berlin Wall

There was snow and ice
on the polished window
too small to see

out of, only winter
garland looped
above the glistening

cobblestones, the small
white lights scattered
like a measure of stars

we called
forgiveness.

III

Green Cards, Promises,

& the Berlin Wall

Green Cards, Promises, & the Berlin Wall

one

> *Come together,* they chanted, *the border is falling*
> *apart between us.* You said "it was beautiful
> in Berlin before the war." *Beautiful,* you were,
> believing the fortune teller who arrived after the war.
> She saw green cards & promises, sunlight falling
> on the face of the New York Harbor. You wore
> a bronzed butterfly in your hair, the crystal necklace
> (gift from my GI father) hovering like a chunk of
> sunlight, radiant, above your breasts. It was
> a shining moment & you believed America was *the pure*
> *dream*—my face, a dark moon surfacing between your
> thighs.

two

Who is it that tells us we are *beautiful*?

three

I dreamed a branch of ocotillo fell on the face
of the Arizona desert.

four

Were you always the most rebellious? Your sister said
you "got the most whippings," youngest daughter
bearing me, illegitimate daughter, I still carry your sin
in the unrelenting heat of this Sonoran desert. At dusk
it is dark with shadows, but mostly the unrelenting
heat. Was it twenty illegals who died this summer,
this side of the border? "Got what they deserved,"
he told me, my neighbor who reminds me of *Opa*
tapping his story of superiority. "Too dangerous
in that country," he warned.

     When I was born,
vesper sparrows fluttered above the German farm
fields, and he spit on you, your penance to birth me
without analgesics. The Sisters of Mercy decided & you
decided to leave the *fatherland,* applied for our
alien registration cards, "green and Christmas was
coming." You said, "The Berlin Wall was a place
to leave bad dreams and your telephone number,"
like the black numbers riding the forearm
of Bob, my Jewish stepfather.

five

"How could you fall in love with a Jew?" your father
dipped the words thin as crepe batter; you will not be
allowed to enter the place of crematoriums & your mother
fried the flowers, anyway. They were the *Holderblumen*
sweet in June, and you were "the one who never appreciated
such a delicacy," those snowy flowers curling up
in hot oil. Like tiny fists cruel & very sweet. "Here,
I will give you one," your mother said.

six

My alien registration card is tattooed with red numbers—
6828607. *Where were you before the Holocaust?*

seven

"What happened to your arm?" asked Karin,
little sister. "Oh, I'm so forgetful, honey, that's
my telephone number," said Bob & we passed
the potatoes around the supper table.

eight

Foreigners continue to visit the Wall & pick fragments
they believe to be genuine. "Don't let them trick you,
it's all gone, not a stone left," Mitzi told me in Berlin,
1992. "Here's the real thing. Take one," and she opened
a box of shards, flecks of paint spattered
red on the white.

nine

Come together, they chanted at the Wall falling down.
How do you say *come together* in German? They called
you "a spy," too beautiful for the barrio of south
Phoenix, "Marlene Dietrich girl." You left
your darkness at the Wall, tried to forget you were
the daughter of a poultry businessman gone bankrupt,
your father twisting the necks of doves & shipping
them quickly to Garmisch where the rich—
between WWI and WWII—enjoyed
the fine things in life.

ten

Lines & creases etched the small mistakes on your face.
"You were the one," my father said. And you bore
me—dark daughter, *mojada* still swimming the harbor.
I have cleared the rubble of stones, Berlin hailed
as *the new capital*. Reconciliation. *Come together,*
the border people are singing, our mothers dreaming
in glass caskets for another hundred years. We are riding
ships on the Rhine & I am crossing blue mountains,
water—a wetback escaping to an American education.

eleven

> *Come together, come together,* they are singing
> at the Gate, from east to west, north
> to south—the messenger-flowers,
> the dead, the ghosts, the cruel
> & the kind, the black shirts,
> brown shirts, the terrifying
> & beautiful angels
> of the four directions—
> *come together over me.*

twelve

Mother, are you listening? Did you take a picture
of the Wall before it all came down, down,
& down?

Train, 1941

The boxcars
clack slowly—
south, through

Heilbronn, Stuttgart,
Göppingen, Ulm,
Neu-Ulm, Augsburg

to Dachau, gray
morning, my mother—
a girl of twelve

shaking rugs
at the upstairs
window. Inside,

the clean house—
no Star of David;
outside, the hot

scent of iron
rocking the tracks,
wheel of memory,

spin of misery.
*What could we have
been more faithful to?*

I would ask her, now;
ask for a ticket out
of that smoke-filled

country. Still, the dependable
timetable of those trains—
another & another

and still, the girl
keeps shaking
rugs at the window.

Cordate Envoy

A strong yellow vein runs down its center.
Flared from that point of balance,
regimented lines cut like shafts of arrows
or furrows of the fields my mother harvested.
Brown spots, small imperfections, rise
on this leaf—like the ones I will carry
on the surface of my own hands.
I raise it to late afternoon sun,
turn it to see pinholes of light,
those places where wind
or the smallest pebble of grief
broke through.

Notes

Sophie and the White Rose
The spring of 1943 was especially significant—the Bermuda conference (to discuss rescue proposals for Europe's Jews) was held on April 19. Eleven days after the conference, William Langer of North Dakota reported that two million Jews in Europe had already been killed.

Firestorm
In J.R.R. Tolkien's *Lord of the Rings* trilogy, Gandalf the Gray falls into the Crack of Doom and disappears into the fire. Transformed, he re-emerges as Gandalf the White because he has been "burned back to the bone." Gandalf the White, Wizard of the Inferno, symbolizes the purity of bone, a state in which everything else has been stripped away.

Salzbergwerk: The Salt Mines Tour
Anna Karolina Sohr, my maternal grandmother, married Alois Kramer. They had seven children—Ana, Luis, Teresia (Resl), Joseph (Sep), Friedrich (Fritz), Maria (Ria, my mother), and Georg.

Schutzstaffel, SS Uncle
The *Schutzstaffel,* or "Black shirts," were Hitler's elite guard. With Nazi regional chiefs, the SS set up, inspected, and commanded the concentration camps. The SS were tattooed with a special number to mark their status. Max, a Holocaust survivor, told me, "They got a tattoo in the armpit."

Those Red Tulips
Three thousand men with typhus were taken out of Dachau, sent away, and gassed between February and December 1942.

Green Morning in the Summer Forest
Green was the medieval color of hope.

About My Mother's Ashes
The Seven-Tabled Forest, Siebentischwald, in Augsburg received its name from a beer tavern that had once been located in the forest and that had seven tables.

Green Cards, Promises, & the Berlin Wall
Holderblumen, elderflower, a shrub that blooms with white flowers in June, is also known as *Holunderblüten. Blüte,* meaning "flower," implies the prime or heyday of life.

GLOSSARY

Bayerischen Wald. Bavarian forest.

Donau. The Danube River.

edelweiss. A delicate white flower that grows high in the Alps.

Knödel. Dumplings.

Kurgarten. A healing garden in a health resort.

La Llorona. The "Weeping Woman," a popular Mexican folktale.

Marktplatz. A marketplace in the heart of a city.

mit Rahmsosse. With cream gravy.

Oblaten. Sweet, waferlike cookies.

Opa. German grandfather.

Schutzstaffel. The "Black Shirts," Hilter's elite guard.

Stadtmarkt. The town market.

Vogelmarkt. Bird market.

Acknowledgments

Grateful acknowledgment is made to the following books and journals, in which some of the poems previously appeared:

Alligator Juniper: "Maria on the High Wire" (winner of the 2002 *Alligator Juniper* award for poetry).

e magazine, special issue: The 1998 Emily Dickinson Award Anthology: "Marlene Dietrich, Rita Hayworth, & My Mother"

Fennel Stalk: "The Red Door" and "First Light"

¡Floricanto Sí! A Collection of Latina Poetry: "The Leaving"

Frontiers: A Journal of Women's Studies: "Salzbergwerk: The Salt Mines Tour" and "High Summer"

The Guadalupe Review: "I Am the Daughter"

Neuste Chicano-Lyrik / Recent Chicano Poetry: "Kleine Gesten, Small Gestures" (German translation at the University of Bamberg)

New Chicana/o Writing, vol. 2: "Embroidering"

New Chicana/o Writing, vol. 3: "Grenze" and "Memorial"

"Embroidering" also appeared in *Glencoe Literature* (Texas edition, 2000).

I would also like to thank the Ucross Foundation, the Millay Colony for the Arts, the Mary Anderson Center, Centrum, the Vermont Studio Center, and the Amazon Foundation for providing support and a "room of one's own" while many of these poems were being written. My appreciation also goes to the Arizona Commission on the Arts and the Tucson-Pima Arts Council. I am especially grateful to Rebecca Seiferle, Barrie Ryan, Alicia Gaspar de Alba, and Demetria Martínez for the careful readings of my poems. Also, I deeply appreciate Laure-Ann Bosselaar and Jane Hirshfield for their help with final revisions while I was in residence at the Vermont Studio Center. Thank you to Karen Falkenstrom for helping prepare my manuscript. And to Maximillian Kowler, who helped with German translations, *vielen Dank!*

About the Author

RITA MARIA MAGDALENO was born in Augsburg, Germany. The daughter of a Mexican American father from Aguas Calientes, Mexico, and a German war-bride mother, she grew up in Marcos de Niza, southside Phoenix. Her poems and stories reflect the diversity of family and cultural experiences.

Magdaleno has lived in Arizona since she was one year old. She works as a Poet in the Schools for the Arizona Commission on the Arts, teaching creative writing to children in Arizona schools. Magdaleno has also conducted writing workshops in Mexico and has helped children create their first exhibit of family stories for the Museo de los Niños in Oaxaca. In 1995, she directed Cuentos y Memorias, an oral history project on Miami, Arizona. The work became a traveling exhibit of photos and oral history stories about Mexican Americans, including her paternal family, who immigrated to Arizona in the 1920s and worked in the copper mines.

Magdaleno has been a Writing Fellow at Millay Colony for the Arts, in New York; the Ucross Foundation, in Wyoming; and the Vermont Studio Center. Her poems appear in *¡Floricanto Sí! A Collection of Latina Poetry* and *Fever Dreams: Contemporary Arizona Poets.* She lives in Tucson with her son Chris, daughter Regina, daughter-in-law Katie, granddaughter Hannah, and her golden lab Pachita.